99 1/2 School Jokes, Riddles, & Nonsense

Written and illustrated
by Holly Kowitt

SCHOLASTIC INC.
NEW YORK TORONTO LONDON AUCKLAND SYDNEY

ISBN 0-590-93775-8

12 11 10 23/0

Printed in the U.S.A. 40

First Scholastic printing, September 1996

For Alan
King of Swing

Gym-nausium

Why did the tiger lose the relay race?

Because the other guy was a terrible cheetah.

Why didn't the coach trust his team?

There were too many sneakers in the locker room.

What is the basketball team doing for breakfast?

Dunking doughnuts.

What happened when the shirts played the jackets?

It ended in a tie.

What's a grasshopper's favorite sport?

Cricket.

What's Tom Thumb's favorite sport?

Miniature golf.

What's a couch potato's favorite sport?

Channel surfing.

Why did the coach put a chicken in the outfield?

To catch fowl balls.

What do bugs sing at baseball games?

The national ant-them.

Let's Do Lunch

Did you hear about the corn who tried to beat up the spinach?

It got creamed.

What kind of cake can you get at the cafeteria?

A stomachache.

Principal: Will you pass the mustard?
Teacher: No, I think I'll flunk it.

Did you see the cereal box and the fruit punch?

Now <u>that's</u> what I call a food fight.

How tough is the meat?

It just challenged me to a fight after school.

Steve: What is it?
Cook: It's bean casserole.
Steve: Yes, but what is it now?

SCHOOL
PICNIC
SPOT
50 MILLION INSECTS
CAN'T BE WRONG

Teacher Creatures

Why did the math teacher cry on the last day of school?

He hates to be divided from his class.

When does a teacher carry birdseed?

When she has a parrot-teacher conference.

Have you ever seen the teachers' lounge?

Only when they're on vacation.

Why did the teacher jump in the lake?

She wanted to test the waters.

Computer Bytes

Why do lumberjacks like computers?

They get to log on.

How did the gnat send the ant a computer message?

By flea-mail.

Why did Spiderman get a computer?

To find the World Wide Web.

What do cats like about computers?

Pushing around a mouse.

I thought you said to bring a ruler!

That's School

What do hams wear in the fall?

Their new school cloves.

Where do they teach you to cook bad food?

Home Eeeecchh.

Why do mummies go to school?

To get a dead-ucation.

MONSTERS AT SCHOOL
What happened to the teacher?
I ate him
Well, there's only one thing left to do, I guess
Cook with substitutes!

Teacher: Have you finished that fifty-page book yet?
Monster: No, I wasn't that hungry.

School Nurse: Was it something you ate?
Sea Monster: Musta been the fish 'n' ships.

MONSTER'S FIRST DAY OF SCHOOL
Well dear, what did you think of the new teacher?
Not bad.
BURP!
What's for dessert?

Book Shelf

Putting Gum Under the Desk
by Wadsworth Saving

Tell the Teacher You Love Her Hairdo
by Lilac A. Rugg

Staying Home with a Cold
by Fay King

Tofu Medley for Lunch Again
by Major Bummer

Knock-Knocks

Knock-knock.
Who's there?
Wanda.
Wanda who?
Wanda start a food fight?

Knock-knock.
Who's there?
Mister E.
Mister E. who?
Mister E. Meat's for lunch today!

Knock-knock.
Who's there?
Wooden.
Wooden who?
Wooden eat the meatloaf if I were you.

Knock-knock.
Who's there?
Gladys.
Gladys who?
Gladys lunch is finally over!

Cleaning Up

What did the school janitor say to the wall?

"One more crack like that and I'll plaster you."

Why did the teacher marry the janitor?

He swept her off her feet.

Why do janitors get in trouble with their parents?

Because they always have to stay after school.

Have You Ever Seen...?

A Film Strip

A Pencil Point

A Lunch Box

A Fire Drill

A Finger Paint

A School Dance

School Nurse

What kind of medicine does a sick headmaster take?

A Princi-pill.

Where did the teacher send the Viking when he got sick in class?

To the school Norse.

Randy: I just swallowed my lunch money!
Nurse: Are you choking?
Randy: No, I'm serious.

Tim: I was playing my harmonica and I swallowed it!
Nurse: At least you weren't playing the piano.

What Happened?

What happened to the bungee jumper who went back to school?

He was suspended.

What happened to the garbageman who went back to school?

He was thrown out.

What happened to the witch who went back to school?

She was ex-spelled.

What happened to the football player who went back to school?

He barely passed.

JOE'S FRUITS
I'd like an apple for my teacher
Sorry, kid- we don't do trades

Different Kinds of School

Why did they give that guy a scholarship to baking school?

He kneaded the dough.

How'd he do?

He made the honor roll.

What kind of tests do they give at beauty school?

Make-up exams.

How do babies cheat at nursery school?

Crib notes.

How do you finish barber school in a week?

By learning all the shortcuts.

Different Kinds of School

Knight School

High School

Sundae School

Finishing School

Homework

What do pigs do after school?

Hamwork.

What do trolls do after school?

Gnomework.

What do barbers do after school?

Combwork.

Art-to-Art

What do Popsicle sticks do in art class?

Make boxes out of people.

What do fish like to paint with?

Watercolors.

Getting There

Mom: Why didn't you take the bus home?
Andy: I tried, but I couldn't fit it into my backpack.

Who can hold up a school bus with one hand?

A crossing guard.

Who has webbed feet and gets good grades?

The class vale-duck-torian.

Where does Bambi go after nursery school?

Kin-deer-garten.

What happens when you bring exotic animals to a school assembly?

It's panda-monium.

Why do chickens do tons of homework?

For eggs-tra credit.

Why did they let the chicken in the school band?

Because he had his own drumsticks.

Where do elephants find their class picture?

In the high school ear book.

The Dog Ate My Homework

What excuse did the nurse give her teacher?

The doc ate my homework.

What excuse did the deer give his teacher?

The doe ate my homework.

What excuse did the goose give her teacher?

The duck ate my homework.

What excuse did the lighthouse give its teacher?

The fog ate my homework.

What excuse did the lumberjack give his teacher?

The log ate my homework.

What excuse did the fly give her teacher?

The frog ate my homework.

The Principal's Office

Why did the teacher send the chicken to the principal's office?

To make an eggs-ample out of her.

Why did the teacher send the clock to the principal's office?

For tocking too much.

Why did the teacher send the vampire to the principal's office?

Because he had a bat attitude.

How Bad Is the Teacher?

He's so bad, he makes the chalk bored.

He's so bad, he gives aspirins a headache.

He's so bad, his students compare test snores.

How Bad Is the Student?

He's so bad, he has to do extra credit work just to flunk.

He's so bad, his mom comes to PTA meetings in disguise.

He's so bad, he flunked lunch.

Where Do Animals Go in September?

Bug to school.

Bark to school.

Bat to school.

Beak to school.

Meet the World's Toughest Teacher

How tough is she?

She sends other teachers to the principal.

She grades students on fire drills.

Her tests are tougher than the roast beef in the cafeteria.

"Her teacher said to write an essay on a whale."

Kiddie Litter

Why did the bully go to beauty school?

He likes to tease hair.

What do you call a nursery schooler who tells on everybody?

A tottletale.

SCHOOL of FISH
How are your grades?
Just can't seem to get above "C" level
This place gives me a haddock
MOBY DICK
JAWS
WILLIAM SHARKSPEARE

History Hash

Teacher: Why did the British fight the Americans?
Mitch: Because they were revolting.

Teacher: Where did Lincoln write the Gettysburg Address?
Jane: On an envelope!

Teacher: What was Alexander the Great's middle name?
Brad: The.

Teacher: What did George Washington do in the fall?
Beth: His back-to-school chopping.

YOU Fill in the Punchline!

Knock-Knock.
Who's there?
Misty.
Misty who?
Misty bus again, so I had to ______________!